Church Quality

Why Excellence in the Local Church Is Essential for Growth

Author: Patricia S. Lotich

First Edition
Patricia S. Lotich, 2014
Published by Create Space
ISBN: 978-0-9916450-0-8

Smart Church Management
Website: SmartChurchManagement.com
Email: info@smartchurchmanagement.com

Contents

Preface

Quality is one of those terms that at times is very vague, depending on our own frames of reference so let's look at a couple of formal definitions.

Dictionary.com defines quality as *"Character with respect to fineness; high grade, superiority, excellence; degree or standard of excellence."* So, in this definition it looks at doing things **excellently**.

The American Society for Quality (ASQ) defines the term as *"The characteristics of a product or service that bears on its ability to satisfy stated, or implied, needs and a product or service free of deficiencies."*

When we think about product quality, we think about things like a car, a refrigerator, a lawnmower, or maybe a hairdryer. We all like to use products that perform in the way we expected when we bought them. For example, when we buy a car, we expect that car to operate without problems, for at least the warranty period, and hope that it operates without issues for years after that, assuming we do our part by maintaining it.

The service sector views quality very differently because it's more *experientially* based. In other words, people judge service quality based on their *perception* of the experience. For example, when we go to the hospital, we judge the care we receive based on how well the employees communicate with us, how efficient the registration process is, and how polite and caring the staff is.

We judge the *experience* more than the clinical care because (unless we have a clinical background) we don't know whether someone is taking our blood pressure or temperature the correct way. We just know how they treated us during the encounter.

For churches, our customers are the visitors, members, employees, and volunteers, and they judge us based on how we interact with them and how efficient and effective our operations are. Everyone likes organization, efficiency, and excellence. Who more than the church should operate out of a passion for excellence! It's our calling!

Quality management is not a new concept to many industries. As far back as the 13th century, there were established models for managing and improving product quality. A discipline that started in manufacturing migrated to service industries such as hospitality, hotels, and healthcare.

As these industries embrace quality concepts, we as consumers develop higher expectations for positive, error-free service experiences. Whether it's a product free from defects or services that are customer-friendly and offer ease of use, we're constantly raising the bar.

Because of this phenomenon, there's an increased pressure on nonprofit and church organizations to embrace quality concepts. The church has been slow to make these types of changes because of a resistance to corporate business practices spilling over into the church.

This quality movement is now a part of the service sectors, making it even more important for churches to incorporate quality concepts, methods, and processes into how they oversee church operations.

Who more than the church should do things with excellence!

Overview

The book begins with a history of the quality movement. It then explains how it moved into many industries and is moving into religious not-for-profits, whether they're ready or not.

We will then cover a quality improvement methodology, which is a formal process for improvement efforts, and learn how to use one of the many quality improvement tools.

We can take this tool and use it to help solve a church-related problem. Once we do this, you can take this tool back to your church to begin using it!

Chapter 1 – The History of Quality

We can trace quality as far back as the 13th century when craftsmen began organizing into unions, called guilds, to maintain standards of quality. This practice continued, and by the mid-1750s, systems of product inspections started in Great Britain when it manufactured large machines, using hydroelectric power and coal, to do the work craftsmen once did, which led to greater output and a need for more workers. By the early 1800s, this phenomenon expanded and became what we know as the Industrial Revolution.

Early in the 20th century, manufacturers began to incorporate quality processes into work practices. During WWII, the U.S. military inspected products made for the war to ensure the safety of its troops. In an effort to save time and money, they began using sampling techniques (which is inspecting a small number of product units rather than an entire batch), specification standards (which is using agreed-to work instructions based on best practices), and training on statistical process control techniques (which is using data to monitor and control product quality).

After WWII, the quality revolution started in Japan and with the help of two Americans, Joseph Juran and W. Edwards Deming, there was a slight shift in how to achieve quality. Rather than focusing on inspection, there was an emphasis on improving organizational processes through the people who used them, instead of inspections.

By the 1970s, Japan's high quality competition broadsided the U.S. automobile and electronic industries. This caused many U.S. manufacturers to respond by emphasizing not only statistical control methods but also approaches that embraced the entire organization. This ultimately birthed TQM, or total quality management, as a business practice.

Healthcare began to embrace quality approaches to the healthcare process in the early 1990s, and since the turn of the century, quality has moved beyond manufacturing and healthcare and into the service, education, and government sectors.

I believe nonprofit and church organizations are the next group to embrace quality practices in how they manage their resources.

Chapter 2 – Why Care About Quality

Many organizations focus on quality because of the impact that poor quality has on their customers. What these organizations do is measure the frequency of a poor quality outcome and set thresholds for poor quality tolerance with the goal of having zero deficiencies 100 percent of the time.

Seems like a pretty hefty goal, right, which is why so many manufacturing, and now service organizations, use the Six Sigma model for managing quality.

Sigma is a term indicating to what extent a process varies from perfection. It's figured by looking at the number of units processed, divided into the number of defects actually occurring, and multiplied by one million, which results in defects-per-million.

Six Sigma is a management philosophy and belief that it's possible to produce totally defect-free products or services. Anyone with customers wants to produce defect-free products, also!

Why Care About Quality in the Church?

So how does this relate to the church? The church manages God's resources (people, time, and money) and represents Christianity. This responsibility should, of course, mean the church must meet an even higher standard of excellence than other organizations.

There are a lot of great churches out there leading the way on quality. These churches have figured out how to operate with high levels of excellence. They have a clear and compelling mission and help members embrace their mission through teaching and opportunities to participate.

However, the church as a whole has the reputation for being lax about quality. Think about it, how often do you see typos and other errors in the bulletin, untrained volunteers, or unresponsiveness to members?

> "Excellence is not about impressing other people; it is about doing it right because it is the right thing to do."
> Phil Baker

These types of things can discredit the organization and leave skeptics snickering. The unfortunate part of this is when the church is sloppy with what it's trying to do, it validates the perception of those people who may need the church the most.

Paying attention to the little things can have a major impact on the perception of the church. And paying attention to the small details takes hard work, focus, and a commitment to excellence!

I would just ask, how can the church expect the world to take us seriously unless we represent the Father with the excellence that He deserves in everything we do?

Chapter 3 – Church Quality

Managing church quality is really about how you manage your God-given resources, which are people, time, and money. To understand this better, you need to ask a few questions:

- Are you managing your people (employees and volunteers) with the best systems and processes available?
- Do you make sure you spend your time on those things that help further your mission?
- How do you manage the money God provides through someone's donation? Are you deliberate with your spending or haphazard with your financial resources?
- Do you create an inviting environment through the maintenance and aesthetic look of your facilities?
- Do you communicate intentionally and with focus? Do your members, volunteers, and employees understand what you're trying to accomplish? But more important, do they understand why you do what you do?

These are all things you should continuously think about.

Fire Prevention vs. Fire Fighting

Question: Is your organization better at putting fires out or better at fire prevention?

Good quality processes can prevent those recurring fires that we all have to deal with – sometimes on a daily basis. For example, if you get recurring complaints, take the opportunity to put a plan in place to eliminate the source of the complaint instead of getting really good at appeasing the complainers.

This is the difference between fire prevention and fighting fires. Fire prevention focuses on greatly reducing or eliminating the possibility of a fire starting! For instance, if the volunteer department diligently does background checks on all new volunteers, the information could make the organization aware of personal issues that could potentially affect a volunteer's role and possibly safeguard members and children from a potential predator.

The church welcomes everyone, but that doesn't necessarily mean it should put a known predator in the children's ministry. Performing due diligence on the front end of the screening process can help to eliminate issues on the back end.

> Fire prevention focuses on greatly reducing or eliminating the possibility of a fire starting!

Quality is woven into everything we do, and it really is the *how* we do things. It's how we:

- Lead and develop people
- Manage limited resources
- Emphasize training employees and valuable volunteers

- Systematically improve what we do by constantly looking at our systems and processes to ensure they're as efficient and effective as possible
- Approach and solve the problems we deal with every day
- Know that we're doing what we want to do and whether or not we're successful at it
- Measure success
- Gather, study, and make decisions based on our data, asking ourselves, is every decision we make data driven? If not, we may be making some poor decisions.

Quality really is about how to manage church operations!

If you look at your organization from 50,000 feet, you can see how quality ties into to everything you do.

Customer Focus

Starting with the customers (those are the church's members, volunteers, employees, and visitors), use quality tools to ensure you take care of all customer groups. You want to take care of the members because they **fund** the church, you want to take care of the volunteers because they're the **labor** of the church, and you want to take care of the employees because they **facilitate** the process.

> "For your church to grow, you must be nice to people when they show up."
> Rick Warren

But most important, you want to create a friendly and welcoming experience for your visitors. If God sends visitors your way, you want to keep them.

Understanding these important customer groups, and developing strategies to meet the needs of each group, will not only help to strengthen the core but also grow the church.

Do you solicit feedback from your customers (members, volunteers, or employees) and ask questions you can use to help you better manage your operation? For example, a church I worked with does a supercharged vacation Bible school every summer. Last year, the camp hosted more than 5000 kids in a two-week period. (Go to **https://jumpkids.com/** to see how they do it.)

When I first started working with them, we had 150 kids, and over the course of 10 years, the camp grew exponentially and requires 1000 volunteers per week to pull it off. We placed a lot of emphasis on our volunteers and always asked for their feedback and gleaned great information about the process of a worker or of a parent, and they offered suggestions that we incorporated to improve the camp each year. It's still a phenomenal success. And, oh, yeah, thousands of kids make a dedication to the Lord each year! What's better than that!

Leadership

Quality takes into consideration your leadership model and how you identify and transfer leadership skills to others. You need to constantly look for ways to develop the next generation of leaders.

This means identifying what leadership abilities you want your leaders to display and creating a system to identify candidates and systematically train them to ensure new leaders are always in development. For instance, some

> "A leader is one who knows the way, goes the way, and shows the way."
> John Maxwell

organizations rotate volunteers out of leadership positions every couple of years in an effort to keep things fresh and to avoid volunteer burnout. Having a process to constantly identify and train leadership allows for smooth transitions.

Resource Management

Every organization has limited resources (people, time, and money), so it's important to establish processes to prioritize the allocation of those resources. For example, creating a church budget allows for intentional use of church financial resources. Or including an analysis of staffing levels (employee or volunteer) when planning a big event can help to ensure the event is manageable and there are enough hands to do the work.

Training and Development

Training and developing the core group of employees and volunteers is critical to ensuring desired behavior, as well as communicating an understanding of job expectations. You should have structured training programs that include all core competencies as defined by the leadership. This can include things like customer service skills, problem solving, conflict resolution in addition to technical skills like computer literacy and organization-specific software programs.

Successful training programs require funding but can have a significant impact on how the organization operates and meets the needs of all of its customer groups. This is a budget item that takes priority.

Process Improvement

It's important to continuously look at internal processes and work to make sure they're as efficient and effective as possible.

> "Every system is perfectly designed to achieve exactly the results it gets."
> Donald Berwick, M.D.

Donald Berwick is a pediatrician who led the quality movement into the healthcare industry in the 1990s, and he said, "Every system is perfectly designed to achieve exactly the results it gets."

What he meant was a bad system will produce bad results every time, and a good system will produce good results. A good employee put in a bad system will have bad results. but the same employee put in a good system will have great results. For example, if the process to drive onto and off your church campus is slow week after week, visitors and even members may get frustrated. And, unfortunately, sometimes they even vote with their feet. The worst part is it's often the parking volunteers who have to deal with the bad process, which creates a negative experience for them.

Data Management

Data provides us with information about how the organization operates, and gathering and using this data can help us make better-informed decisions.

I used to tell my employees, "If I don't know it's broke, I can't fix

> You can't manage what you don't measure.

it." What I meant by this was unless I'm (you're) aware of the issues, we can't find a solution. Whether the issue is a lack of resources to pull off a big event or declining weekly attendance, you need to address both and put a plan in place to address these problems.

With the easy access to computer systems, most times finding available data is pretty easy. However, there are times when you need to collect data manually. For example, if the children's ministry has a minimum worker to child ratio, and the children's church has to turn away kids because there aren't enough volunteers to staff it, you need some sort of tracking mechanism to collect this data. Once you collect the data, it gives the children's ministry coordinator the information needed to solicit help and support from church leadership.

Organizational Assessment

Once you decide to develop a quality management program, the first step is an organizational assessment. You can do this in-house or by using an objective third party consultant. The goal of the assessment is to provide information about the organization and to identify areas that need focused planning and attention.

When doing an assessment, some things you should discuss are finances, resource allocation, leadership, customer experience, internal processes, training and development, and data management. Sound familiar?

Chapter 4 – Practical Steps

Review and take into consideration every area of the operation. What you want to do is determine where the organization is today, where you'd like to take the organization, and where the gap between these two things is. This is a gap analysis.

To do a gap analysis, you need to look at the organization as a whole and ask some hard questions.

To answer some of these questions, you need to gather some data. I recommend pulling financial data from the last 12 to 24 months, customer feedback data (if you have it), employee feedback, volunteer feedback, church member feedback, church programs, leadership, and process improvement.

A gap analysis answers the question, "Where are we compared to where we want to be?" The process looks at the vision – where do you want to go – and where you are currently. The analysis can be in relation to ministry program development, discipleship, financial viability, or customer experience. The gap analysis process identifies and targets all areas. An example of a church's current state:

> Where are we compared to where we want to be?

The church is renting a temporary facility until it can build a permanent building; the church lacks volunteer leadership; the church children's program doesn't have a weekly curriculum; the church has no process for discipleship, the volunteer application process is too long and cumbersome, there's declining membership, donations are down, employee turnover is high, the facility is old.

Some questions to ask yourselves:

- [ ] What is our mission and vision? Is it in writing and available to church members, volunteers, and employees?
- [ ] What are our guiding principles and core values? Are they in writing, and do members, volunteers, and employees understand?
- [ ] Do we have a strategy and plan to achieve our mission?
- [ ] What is our budgeting process, and how do we allocate church revenues?
  - Does our budget break even? If no, how do we deal with budget variances?
  - Do we budget for growth/future expansion?
  - Do we budget for the unexpected?
- [ ] Does the budget support the mission and strategy? Do we budget resources to support and grow key programs? Do we budget for facility enhancements?
- [ ] How do employees spend their time? Do they understand what's expected of them? Is what they're spending their time on supporting the mission and strategy? Or, are they spending time on things that add no value?

- [ ] Are employees in the right roles? Are they using their unique gifts? Is there a process to train, transfer, or terminate? Do we carry employees on the payroll that add no value to the organization?
- [ ] What is our process to recruit and hire the best and brightest?
- [ ] How do volunteers spend their time? Do they understand what's expected of them? Is what they're spending their time on supporting the mission and strategy?

> "Get the right people on the bus, the wrong people off the bus, the right people in the right seats and then figure out where to drive."
> Jim Collins

- [ ] Are volunteers in their right roles? Are we using their unique gifts wisely?
- [ ] What is our process to train and develop volunteers?
- [ ] How do we know our customers (members, volunteers, and employees) have a good experience?
- [ ] Do we monitor customer satisfaction?
  - o Do we systematically solicit feedback from our customers (members, volunteers, and employees)?
  - o Do we have a systematic approach to responding to customer issues?

- o Do we create improvement plans based on customer feedback?
- ☐ What is our process for problem solving?
- ☐ Does employee and volunteer behavior reflect our core values? Do they understand and follow our internal policies and procedures? Do we audit them?
- ☐ What is our process for identifying potential leaders?
- ☐ What does leadership development look like in our environment?
- ☐ What are the things people (members, volunteers, and employees) complain about?
- ☐ Does the space we have adequately accommodate our members and visitors at our weekly services?
- ☐ How do we use technology to further our mission?
- ☐ Do visitors to our church understand what we're trying to accomplish, and are they excited to join in? When people visit your church, do they quickly understand what you are about and what you are trying to accomplish? Often, visitors are in and out, and you aren't even aware they were there, so making that first impression a positive one is very important.
- ☐ Is church attendance stagnant or growing? What's our plan to address either stagnation or growth?

- How is church attendance? Rick Warren says, *"**If a church is not growing, it is dying.**"* Stagnation often leads to decline. Are you paying attention?
- If the church is growing, is the church budgeting for a church expansion?

☐ How efficient is the process to identify, approve, train, and place volunteers in their roles?

> "If a church is not growing, it is dying."
> Rick Warren

- Ask the question, how do we take care of volunteers? Is the process to manage them efficient, is their training effective, and are they serving in the best role for their particular gifts?

These are all questions that can help create a gap analysis and, ultimately, affect the quality of church operations.

Example of a current state:

- Church attendance has declined by 10 percent during the last 12 months.
- Volunteer satisfaction scores are at 72 percent.
- Youth attendance: 60 percent of teenagers 13 to 18 years old attend the youth program.
- The church worship center is at 85 percent capacity week after week.
- The children's church has grown by 25 percent in two years.

- The church has been over budget by 8 percent for the past two years.

Once you clarify the current state, you can compare it to where you'd like the church to be and put a plan in place to bridge that gap. Understanding the gap is the reality check. The first steps in solving problems is **identifying** them, **acknowledging** them, and putting a **plan** in place to fix them.

Chapter 5 – Principles of Quality

There are principles of quality that look at how the organization manages itself and asks the questions:

- Are we doing the **right** things? In other words, is our focus on doing those things that get us closer to achieving our mission?

and,

- Are we doing things the **right way?** This means are we **efficient and effective** in what we're trying to accomplish.

- Are we doing these **right things** (mission-focused) the **right way** (efficiently and effectively) the **first time** and every time to ensure predictable results.

> "Efficiency is doing things right; effectiveness is doing the right things."
> Peter Drucker

For example:

Are we doing the *right* things?

What are we spending our time and resources on?

Do these things help us achieve our mission?

Are we doing things *right*?

Have we found the best (**right**) way to do those things that help us achieve our mission? How do we ensure that we're doing things efficiently and effectively?

Are we doing the *right* things *right* the **first** time?

For example, once we determine our priorities and our approach, can we achieve this the first time (and every time)?

Let's say we determined that a priority is to make visitors feel welcomed. We develop a process to identify and reach out to church visitors. So we need to ask ourselves, is our approach to doing this consistent every time we interact with a visitor?

How Do We Decide What the *Right* Things Are?

The strategy of the organization determines the right things. The strategy supports the vision and the mission. This is when having a written vision and mission statement is so important. When the organization can articulate what its

> "Change requires vision. Sustained vision requires leadership. Leadership is a gift."
> Andy Stanley

purpose is (mission) and what it's trying to achieve (vision), it can guide decision-making and prioritize the use of resources (people, time, and money).

The strategy maps out the steps to achieve the mission, and it's those tactical steps that determine the *right things* to do. For example, let's say your organization has a strategic objective to reach teenagers between the ages of 13 and 19. The question is whether the church should spend resources on a youth facility and sound equipment. To answer this simple question, ask a second question. What is our mission and how does this initiative support our mission? If the answer is yes, then commit to and budget the resources, and if not, the answer is a simple no.

How Do We Know Whether We're Doing Things *Right*?

Doing things right means having a systematic approach to ensuring we offer products or services the right way – and with excellence.

The level of commitment to create standards (how do we do things), training (employees/volunteers) on those standards, and to hold people accountable for adhering to those standards determines excellence. For example, let's say there's a strategic objective to make visitors feel welcomed and comfortable when visiting your church. You developed service standards and trained

> "Embracing an agreed upon standard of excellence is how you create a culture."
> Andy Stanley

volunteers to demonstrate welcoming behaviors – being friendly, smiling, and engaging. Once everyone agrees on these standards, and someone trains the employees/volunteers, a church leader should mentor and coach them to ensure consistency in practice. This consistency is what creates excellence when doing those **right** things **right**.

How Do We Do the *Right* Things *Right*, the *First* Time and Every Time?

We've identified what the **right** things are. And we've talked about doing things the **right way**, but how do we do that the first time and every time?

Consistency comes from training, observation, coaching, and reminders. We can all relate to learning something – a new skill. We do it for a while and over time get lazy, look for shortcuts, or just forget the correct way of doing things.

Schedule time with your leadership team to do an annual review of policies and procedures. Take the time to modify and update them as trends, priorities, and strategy changes. Then, schedule annual refreshers with employees and volunteers. Investing the time to conduct annual refreshers is just good business practice.

> "If you don't define what excellence looks like for your staff and volunteers, they will define it for themselves."
> Andy Stanley

Also, take the time to review policies, procedures, and standards as part of ongoing training for employees and volunteers. As part of the training, remind people of the why behind what you do. For example, remind volunteers that when they welcome a new baby and mom to the children's church, they're helping the mother feel comfortable handing her child over to a stranger and possibly offering her the opportunity to sit in church without distraction or interruption. This simple act could have a significant impact on the life of a busy mom. This is why helping employees and volunteers remember **why** they do what they do is so very important.

Chapter 6 – Continuous Improvement

Creating a culture of continuous improvement requires having an *AIM* or knowing exactly what the organization is striving for. This means the entire organization should understand the concept of excellence and continually look for ways to do things better and more efficiently, resulting in higher levels of effectiveness.

When everyone understands the aim of excellence, there's a synergy to achieve that objective. Excellence doesn't just happen; it's intentional!

> "Be a yardstick of quality. Some people aren't used to an environment where excellence is expected."
> Steve Jobs

To achieve excellence, you need a systematic approach to improvement initiatives that result in positive change for the organization.

FOCUS PDCA Improvement Methodology

We now understand why improvement and a focus on excellence are important, so what we need is a method to use to help with our improvement efforts.

FOCUS PDCA is a methodology that many organizations use to guide their improvement efforts. It's simply a formalized process for improvement.

Organizations use the FOCUS PDCA methodology for several reasons.

- It's user friendly and does not require a lot of technical or scientific knowledge. It's easy to learn quickly, and with time and practice, skills can increase.

- It's a methodology that helps to keep everyone focused on the improvement effort. The structure of the process encourages focus and accountability for completing assigned tasks.

- It gets employees (and volunteers) involved in the process of problem solving. This improvement model places value on the wisdom and experience of front-line workers (employees or volunteers) and encourages the use of their expertise.

- It provides a plan and steps for improvements. These plans help to eliminate the frustrations that come with working in an environment that allows organizational problems to dictate internal processes, instead of the opposite.

- It's a methodology that uses data to ask the questions and has tools to help determine the steps toward improvements.

- Organizations use this methodology because it works!

So what does **FOCUS PDCA** mean? It is actually an acronym for an approach to problem-solving and it stands for:

FOCUS

Find

Organize

Clarify

Understand

Select

> "Everything that is currently in place was adopted as an improvement over an outdated approach that was at one time a revolutionary idea."
> Andy Stanley

Now let's go through each one to understand its meaning.

Find a process or identify a problem that needs improvement. Problems are pretty easy to identify. Just think about the chronic complaints you get or those things that simply frustrate you at work. Those things that impact church customers (members, volunteers, and employees) or internal processes that make it difficult to do things.

For example, if new volunteers are continually venting frustration about the length of time it takes to go through the volunteer application, approval, and placement process, it's probably time to work toward streamlining the process.

Organize a team that understands or works with the process or problem. The team consists of people who know the process well and can speak to what works and what needs changing. For example, if you want to improve the volunteer application process, you need a team that includes the people who administer the process as well as people who experience the process – new volunteers.

Clarify the knowledge. Clarifying the knowledge of the process can help to ensure there's agreement on what the real issues are. Every person who walks through the process or experiences the problem sees things from a little different perspective making it important to clarify the knowledge from every perspective.

Understand the process variations. There are variations in every process. The trick is to discover what causes the variations so you can minimize the peaks and valleys.

For example, think about how long it takes you to drive to work. There's an average commute time that's calculated by using the actual times it takes every day. Let's say your commute is anywhere from 16 minutes to 24 minutes, depending on traffic and weather conditions. Your average commute time would be 20 minutes and any variation more than four minutes either side is an outlier. In this example, a snow day might make the time vary significantly, but it's still an outlier because it's an unusual (not daily) occurrence.

In the example of the volunteer application process, to understand process variations, you need to collect some baseline (before) data so you can track the length of time it takes to process a volunteer. This involves collecting data starting from the date you receive the application to the date the volunteer has a position and a schedule to work. Use this baseline data later as a measure to see whether the improvements resulted in a positive change.

Select a solution to test. Have the team determine what solution you'd like to test and create a goal for the improvement. For instance, streamlining the volunteer application process time might result in a team goal that reduces the volunteer application processing time from six weeks to seven days. This gives the team a specific AIM and goal to work toward.

PDCA

Plan

Do

Check

Act

Repeat

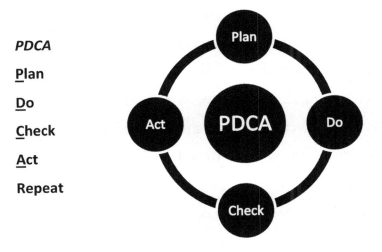

After there's an understanding of the problem, and you selected a solution, it's time to:

Plan the improvement effort. You do this by creating an action-plan for team members to implement. Creating an action plan requires identifying all the necessary tactical steps, assigning accountability or responsibility for each step, and creating a timeline for completion. This action plan document is what you use to monitor progress and hold team members accountable for achieving objectives.

Do the plan. You do this by completing the steps in the action plan and holding people accountable for assigned steps and timelines. This is the most critical step in the entire improvement process. If people do not follow through with the **Do**, the plan is nothing more than a piece of paper.

Check the results to see whether the improvement efforts truly made a difference. In the volunteer application process example, it's important to have the baseline data showing the actual length of the process **prior** to the improvement efforts as a measure to monitor progress. Collect the same data after the improvements are in effect and compare the before and after process times to determine whether the efforts resulted in the goal or AIM of the efforts.

And finally, you're going to **Act** on those results. If the improvements worked, write the policy, train the people who work with the process, and continue to monitor.

In the volunteer application process, update the policy for processing new volunteers, train the volunteer department on the new process, and communicate the new expectations for volunteer processing times. Once those who work with the process receive training, you'll monitor how the process is working and help to fine-tune the process.

If the improvement effort didn't work, you go through the process again. **Repeating** the cycle is how continuous improvement works!

Find a Process to Improve

When you're trying to determine what process or problem to tackle, you need to ask yourselves some questions that can help steer you toward the best opportunity to tackle. This is when you can determine whether this is the right thing to spend limited resources (people, time, and money) on.

OK, let's look at some questions to ask yourselves.

- What need led to the selection of this process/problem?
- What data is available to support this selection? (How will we know we improved?)
- What do we want to get out of this effort (AIM)?
- Who are the customers of this process?
- How does this process or problem impact our customers?
- How does this effort tie to our priorities?

Now let's go through each of these questions one at a time to get a better understanding.

What need led to the selection of this process?

Was the need obvious through complaints or other customer (member, volunteer, and employee) input? Or was the need identified through strategic objectives?

What data is available to support this selection? (How will we know we improved?)

Is there data to support the selection? For example, you may get several complaints about the campus parking, but it's important

> "It is a capital mistake to theorize before one has data."
> Arthur Conan Doyle

to do a little study and collect some info to validate those complaints.

What do we want to get out of this effort?

Next, you need to decide what you want to get out of this improvement effort. With data, you can see the baseline going into the process and set a goal for the outcome of your improvement efforts. For instance, if the perceived and real traffic flow issue (based on the collected data) is that it takes someone an average of eight minutes to get off the parking lot during peak hours, then you could set a goal to get people off the parking lot in four minutes, on average. You need a target goal, based on the data collected, so you can go back and demonstrate that the improvement worked.

Who are the customers of this process?

You need to consider who the customers of the process are. In this example, it's the members, visitors, and parking volunteers. (They're the ones who hear the complaints.) Then, look to see how the problem affects those customers.

How does this process or problem affect our customers?

It affects the volunteer who deals with complaining members who have difficulty parking week after week. The parking process also impacts the member who has to get to work right after church. The problem has an effect on both but in very different ways.

How does this effort tie to our priorities?

Look at the organization's mission, vision, and values to determine this. What is the strategy for achieving the mission, and the question to ask is, is good traffic flow important to the experience we're trying to create? I would say, in most cases, yes.

> "We see our customers as invited guests to a party, and we are the hosts. It's our job every day to make every important aspect of the customer experience a little bit better."
> Jeff Bezos

Organize a Team

Questions:

- Does the team membership represent the process? (Are all the key stakeholders present?)

- Is the team's knowledge aligned with the improvement opportunity?
- Do team members understand the time commitment?

Next, you can organize a team.

Does the team membership represent the process? (Are all the key stakeholders present?)

This team should include people who work within the process. Using the experiences of these people helps to bring a fresh perspective that we often don't get from the church office.

> "Winning teams have players that make things happen."
> John Maxwell

Is the team's knowledge aligned with the improvement opportunity?

The team should represent a broad knowledge base and understanding of the problem. For example, the parking volunteers or a random church member who gets stuck in the traffic flow represent different perspectives. So, they should join the team.

Do team members understand the time commitment?

Be sure to pick team members who have the interest and the time available to help with the improvement efforts.

For example, share expectations for the days and times the team will meet, how often the team will meet, and the estimated time it will take the team to achieve its AIM. It is only fair to make people (especially volunteers) aware of what they are committing to. The last thing you want is team members who bail in the middle of the project because the time commitment was more than they anticipated.

Clarify the Knowledge

Flow chart the actual process

When there's a defined process, take the time to create a flowchart or picture to provide the team with a visual of how the process looks. It's amazing how different steps look in picture format as compared to merely talking about them.

In the following example, the process shows the steps a parent must take to drop a child off with the children's ministry. It shows how a new child will have a slightly longer process than a child already registered with the children's church.

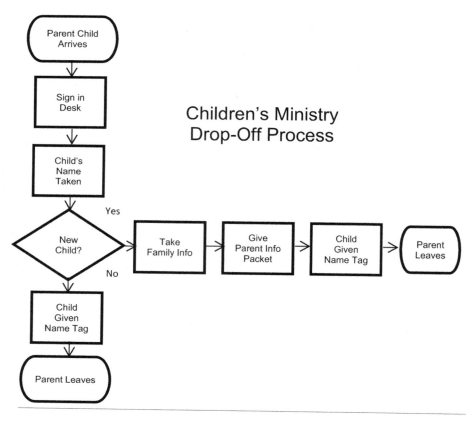

Do all team members view the actual process the same?

In this example, make sure employees, volunteers, and parents all agree with the process as drawn. If a parent perceives a step that employees and volunteers don't see, the process is not accurate, and you need to add the step to the flow chart so that all team members agree.

Is baseline data available?

The team should determine how to measure or collect data for the process. In other words, how do we know the volunteers follow the steps to this process every time or how long it takes a parent to drop off or register a child? How many children attend the children's church? How many of those who attend are new or visitors and how do you keep track of these numbers?

Understand the Variation

Now, you want to make sure you understand the process variation as well as its capability. For example, you can predict that Easter Sunday will have higher church attendance so the traffic flow is at its peak, but you also need to understand what the campus capabilities are. So if there's only one exit out of the church parking lot, there's a limit to how much improvement you can make to the traffic flow. You also need to understand the qualitative characteristics the customer/church member defines.

So, if a parking volunteer complains about a broken process, you need to try to learn from him to make sure you understand the issues. To do this, you must collect data to validate their expressed concerns.

Select the Improvement

When **selecting** the improvement to test, you need to consider how feasible the option is and what improvements can bring the greatest enhancements to the process and improve the efficiency and effectiveness.

> "Plans are nothing; planning is everything."
> Dwight D. Eisenhower

You want to get the biggest bang for your buck!

Questions:

- What are all the possible improvements?
- What criteria will you use to select one?
  - Most feasible
  - Greatest enhancement
  - Most efficient and effective

The goal is to only invest resources (people, time, and money) on those efforts that have a direct impact on the customers (members, volunteers, and employees) or the efficiency of internal processes. No church has resources to waste on initiatives that add no value. This is why selecting the *right* problem or process to tackle is critical to long-term strategy.

Plan the Improvement

Planning the improvement requires determining what you need to do and putting together a formal plan of action. This includes determining **who** will do **what, when,** and **how.** In addition, you must continue to collect data about the process to ensure the improvements result in a positive change. You also need to determine how to continue to monitor that change over time. Questions:

- What is it you're trying to achieve (AIM)?
- What are the steps that need to happen to achieve your AIM?
- Who's responsible to make each step happen?
- When will you make the changes?
- How should you pilot the change?
- Who, what, where, and how will you collect data?
- How will you monitor the change (very important step) to attain your goal?

Do the Improvement

This step is where the rubber meets the road. This is when you implement your plan and begin to monitor it to make sure the results are what you intended. This step has a lot of accountability attached to it, and it really can make or break the entire effort.

Holding people accountable for completing desired steps is sometimes tricky, particularly when the majority of the team is volunteers. This is why it's so important to select a team that has a passion for the issues and the time to commit to the work. Doing the **Do** is critical to success!

Questions:

- Are you implementing the improvement according to plan?

> "If you don't clarify the win for a team, they will do it themselves." Andy Stanley

- Who is monitoring the plan?

Check the Results

OK, you came up with a plan and you implemented the plan, so now it's time to **check the results**. You do this by looking at your baseline data and comparing it to current results and assessing how the results are now affecting those close to the process.

In other words, did your efforts pay off?

Questions:

- Did the process improve? From the viewpoint of the:
    - ✓ Customer
    - ✓ Those who work within the process
    - ✓ Other stakeholders
- Measurement. How do we know it improved?

Act on the Improvement

- ✓ Standardization of improvement
- ✓ Policies and procedures revised
- ✓ Training

✓ Ownership

✓ Repeat FOCUS - PDCA

Once you make the improvements, you need to standardize the process and write policies and procedures to reflect the changes. You then need to train employees and volunteers on the new process and help them to accept and implement it. This requires ongoing monitoring so employees and volunteers don't slip back into old habits.

If the improvements **did not** give the result you were looking for, repeat the process and test a new improvement opportunity.

Chapter 7 – Problem-Solving Tools

You just learned about the FOCUS PDCA cycle, now you want to look at a problem-solving tool you can pull out of your toolbox and use to help identify necessary improvements and how to plan that improvement.

Problems. It sometimes seems as if we solve one problem and another one pops up right behind it. Why? Because fixing a problem creates new problems! Think about these examples:

> "You have to be smarter than the problem."
> John Stiffler

Problem: A church of 1000 members creates strategies and sets goals to increase membership by 50 percent.

They're successful with their endeavors, and now they have a new problem: not enough seating for the new members and not enough children's ministry space for the increased number of kids.

New problem: We need more space.

The team puts together a recommendation to add another service to take the stress off one weekly service. A second service begins. Problem solved.

New problem: We need more volunteers to operate the second service.

As you can see, those who manage any type of organization are paid to solve problems. The tools they use can vary from gut instincts to structured problem-solving tools. Skilled managers are good problem-solvers and use problem-solving tools to help them find the best solutions.

Any organization that's growing is constantly solving one problem that creates a new problem in need of a solution. Having problems to solve is not necessarily a bad thing, but the solutions are best when they're part of an established problem-solving process.

The secret is having a structured problem-solving process, called total quality management. Quality concepts provide problem-solving tools that can help identify problems and provide ways to solve problems.

> "Quality is never an accident; it is always the result of high intention, sincere effort, intelligent direction and skillful execution; it represents the wise choice of many alternatives."
> William Foster

Quality Problem-Solving Tools

Organizations use quality tools to solve problems and monitor and manage improvement initiatives. There are several types of tools used, but here we'll talk about the most common ones. Different problems call for different tools, and many of those tools have multiple uses.

The trick is to become familiar with and comfortable with all the quality management tools so you can pull the appropriate one out of your toolbox when there's a problem to solve.

5 Whys

One quality problem-solving tool is the "5 Whys." This is an exercise that can quickly drill down to the root cause of a problem. It's tempting to jump to the first conclusion when trying to solve a problem, so it's important to make sure that what you think is the root of the problem truly is. Let's look at this example.

Problem: Children's ministry has to turn away children because there aren't enough workers to comply with teacher-to-student ratios.

Let's look at this problem and ask the question **why** five times.

1. Why? The first answer might be: All the scheduled workers didn't show up for their shifts.
2. Why? When calling the workers who did not show up for their shifts, a few answered, "I didn't know I was scheduled."
3. Why? Workers didn't receive their monthly schedule in the mail.
4. Why? Workers were on the mailing list and their schedules mailed, but they didn't receive the mail.
5. Why? Workers moved but didn't notify the office of address changes.

Now if you look at the answer to the first "why" and stop there, you may have the tendency to lay blame on the workers and jump to the conclusion that these workers are irresponsible and unreliable. But as you dig down into the fourth and fifth why, you will see a clearer picture of the issue.

It's not about the people; it's about the process. If you put good people in bad processes, the outcomes don't improve. When problems arise, it's human nature to try to find the culprit and lay blame on someone, but more times than not the person is working in a broken process that limits his or her ability to perform well.

Let's look at another example. Imagine that you have a receptionist, and you're constantly getting complaints about the fact that she doesn't know the answers

> It's not about the people; it's about the process.

to callers' questions, and she continues to transfer callers to the wrong person or wrong department. You can discipline that employee, or you can try to learn what in the process is not working.

Problem: Complaints about the receptionist not knowing the answer to questions asked.

1. Why? The receptionist doesn't know the answer to questions or gives our wrong information.

2. Why? The receptionist manual does not have accurate answers to common questions.

3. Why? The receptionist manual is not updated as scheduled.

4. Why? Changing information is not given to the receptionist to update the manual.

5. Why? The administrative assistant who takes minutes at the manager's meeting does not pass information along to the receptionist.

6. Why? Administrative assistant was not instructed to do so during a review of her job description.

As you can see from this example, the problem is a training issue, but not with the receptionist, which would not have been identified without asking the question at least 5 times.

Once you separate the person from the problem, you can drill down on the causes and fix the process that will ultimately help the person perform their job duties.

Flowchart

Most of us are familiar with flowcharts. You've seen flowcharts showing relationships within organizational structures. Flowcharts also show how a document process flows. Use this tool when trying to figure out bottlenecks or breakdowns in current processes. Flowcharting the steps of a process gives a picture of what the process looks like and can shed light on issues within the process. Flowcharts also show changes in processes when there are improvements or when there's a new workflow process.

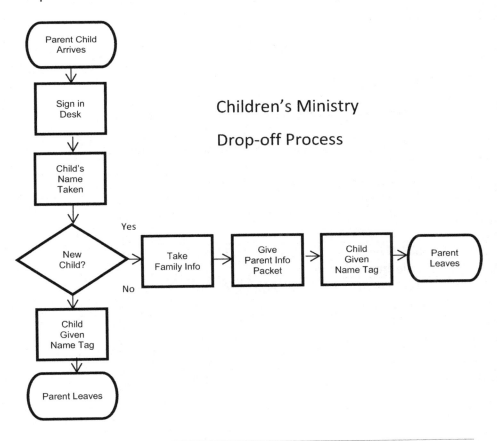

Children's Ministry

Drop-off Process

Check Sheet

A check sheet is a basic quality tool used to collect data. A check sheet can track the number of times a certain incident happens. As an example, a large church that schedules hundreds of volunteers to serve at every church service may track the number of times volunteers don't show up for scheduled shifts. This check sheet would total the number of times a volunteer doesn't report as scheduled when compared to the reasons for the volunteer not showing up.

Check Sheet		
Date: May 10, 20XX		
Problem: Volunteer not showing up as scheduled		
Reason	**Number of Volunteers**	**Subtotal**
Did not receive schedule	///// ///// ///// //	17
Forgot	///// ///// ///	13
Sick/family emergency	///// /////	10
Issue with volunteer role	///// ///	8
Other	////	4
	Total	**52**

Pareto Chart

A Pareto chart is a bar graph of data showing the most frequent occurrences through the least. When looked at from most to the least number of occurrences, it's an easy picture to see how to prioritize improvement efforts. This chart shows the occurrences for volunteers not showing up to work their schedule. The most significant problems stand out, and you can target those first.

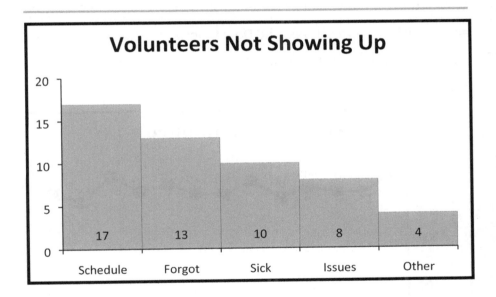

Control Charts

Control charts or run charts plot data points on a line over time and give a picture of data movement. It demonstrates when data is consistent or when there are high or low outliers in occurrences of data.

It focuses on monitoring performance over time by looking at variations in data points. It distinguishes between common cause and special cause variations. The Dow Jones Industrial Average is a good example of a control chart.

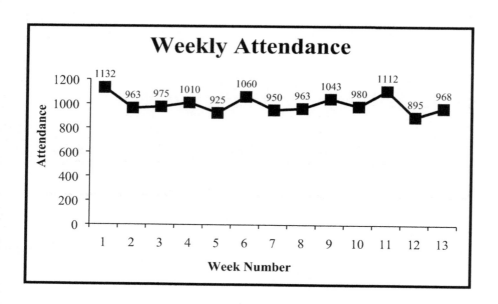

Histogram

A histogram is a bar chart picture that shows patterns in data that fall within typical process conditions. Changes in a process should trigger a new collection of data. For example, the histogram below shows the highest volume of phone calls is about contribution statements. This is a seasonal high number that should redistribute over time.

A minimum of 50 to75 data points will ensure an adequate number of data points. This could mean collecting data on phone calls over several weeks or even months. The patterns demonstrate an analysis that helps understand variation and provides information to use to improve an internal communication process.

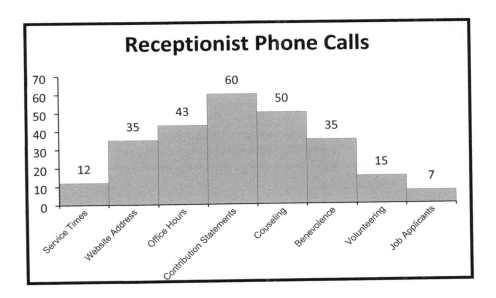

Scatter diagrams

Scatter diagrams are graphs that show the relationship between variables. Variables often represent possible causes and effect.

For instance, a scatter might show how volunteer training affects volunteer satisfaction scores. This diagram shows the relationship between the percentage of volunteers going through a formal orientation process and volunteer satisfaction scores.

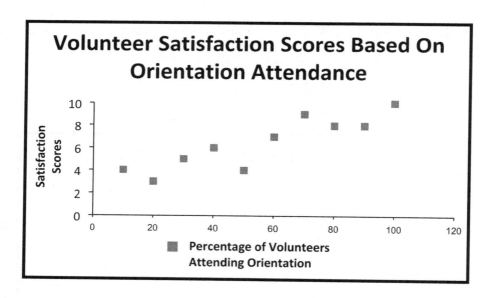

Fishbone – Cause and Effect Diagram

A cause and effect diagram, also known as a fishbone diagram, shows the different causes of a problem. The problem is identified and written in the box (head of the fish) to the right. Then, there's the spine of the fish, and then off the spine are major causes of the problem.

Causes typically go into categories of people, processes, materials, and equipment. Brainstorming with a group familiar with the problem identifies the causes. Once you identify all causes, you can use them to develop an improvement plan to help resolve the identified problem.

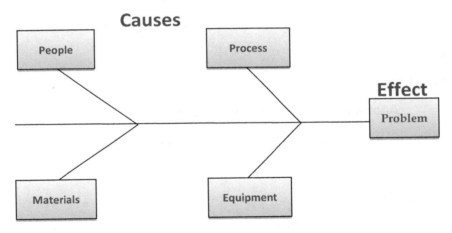

Now keep in mind that these are common categories, but depending on the problem you're trying to solve, the categories may turn out to be very different from these natural groupings.

The goal is to identify a list of issues and put them in their own natural category.

This tool can help us identify some of the driving issues of the problem we're trying to solve.

Every problem has a root cause, something that's driving the problem. What we want to do is try to find out what that is so we can eliminate it.

Let's think about some easy problems we can all relate to and identify the root causes.

Debt

For example, debt. We know that the typical root cause of debt is spending more money than we earn (even though there are times when debt is out of someone's control – job loss, medical care, etc.).

Weight Gain

Another example is weight gain. The typical root cause is consuming more calories than we burn (unless there's an uncontrolled medical condition, certain drugs, etc.).

Being Late for Work

We know that the root cause of being late for work is often sleeping in that extra 15 minutes (however, sometimes it's weather, traffic, or car problems).

The point is, every problem has a root cause, and the goal is to take a hard look and try to determine what the root cause is so you can put a plan in place to eliminate it.

If we can drill down to what the real (not perceived) issue is, we can address the issue at its root and eliminate, or greatly reduce, the problem.

For example, there might be a perception that the root cause of debt is not earning enough money, but the real issue is spending more than is earned. Separating the perception from the real issue is important when trying to get at the root cause.

Problem Classifications

✓ **People** (training, staffing, turnover, rushed, self-discipline)

✓ **Equipment** (capacity, use of space, availability)

✓ **Process/Method** (flow of information/steps in the process)

✓ **Materials** (supplies needed to support process; for instance, brochures).

Most problems fit into natural categories. And from there you can figure out how to address the issues. For example,

- Do the issues relate to training, space capacity, or the supplies?
- Is it equipment, capacity, or use of space?
- Is it a process flow issue?
- Is it the materials required to support the process, for example, a training manual?

These are all questions you need to consider when you try to drill down on a problem.

Each tool has advantages for certain situations, and not all tools are for all problem-solving. Once a tool is learned, you can adapt it for different problem-solving opportunities. As with anything else, using tools properly takes time, practice, and experience.

Chapter 8 – Practice

Let's practice on a real problem and use the fishbone diagram tool to help solve a problem.

Let's say you're having problems with slow traffic flow before and after weekly church services. Now let's see if we can answer the questions and categorize the issues.

Problem: Slow traffic flow before and after church services

Question: What are the people, equipment, processes, and material issues contributing to this problem?

Parking volunteers say they're having a difficult time getting cars on and off the parking lot quickly, frustrating members and visitors.

> "Churches shouldn't do anything that makes it unnecessarily difficult for people who are turning to God."
> Andy Stanley

Feedback from members say, the church has a reputation for having a frustrating parking situation. And the fair weather members and visitors just don't want to deal with it. It's now affecting church attendance.

Now, you have to figure out what's causing these traffic jams.

My pastor used to say he has "prayed for traffic jams on Sunday for years," so in his mind, the problem is not a problem; it's answered prayer!

But all kidding aside, someone who is new to the church may not agree with that!

Now let's pull out those questions mentioned earlier and see whether you selected the right problem to tackle. You have to answer these questions.

- What need led to the selection of this process?
- What data is available to support this selection? (How will we know we improved?)
- What do we want out of this effort?
- Who are the customers of this process?
- How does this impact our customers?
- How does this effort tie to our priorities?

Since traffic flow is a problem, you need to ask:

- What need let to the selection of the traffic flow process?
- What data do we have that shows this is a real (not perceived) problem?
- What's our goal in this improvement effort, or what do we want from our effort to affect positive change?
- Who are the customers of this process?
- Does this effort tie in to our priorities and mission?

Asking these questions helps to make sure you're focusing on "doing the **right** things **right** the **first time.**"

OK, now create a fishbone diagram. But before you can do that, you need to determine what all of the issue categories are. To do this, brainstorm with your team and use any available qualitative data that you have and just start making a list.

What I like to do is an **affinity** exercise. In this exercise, I provide the team with Post-it notes and ask them to put one issue they think is causing the problem on each note. I ask them to work alone on this exercise (to speed up time and eliminate the rabbit trail side conversations). We do this for about five to 10 minutes. I watch the group working and thinking, and I usually know when they're ready.

Once all of the team members have written their Post-it notes, I ask them to take the notes and sort them into natural categories. These categories become the fishbone.

As you can see from this diagram, you identified some issues you think might be contributing to the traffic flow problem. For example some of the issues are:

- There's a shortage of parking cones.
- The signage isn't good.
- Parking volunteers are unclear about assigning parking spots.
- The police who help with traffic flow aren't receiving important information needed to do their jobs.
- The flow of traffic stalls in the main traffic lanes.
- New parking volunteers don't understand parking responsibilities.

- The service times run too close together.

- There aren't enough parking volunteers to manage the flow of traffic.

- There aren't enough available parking spots.

- There's only one entrance and one exit, which has a significant impact on the inflow and outflow of traffic.

As you can see, we've sorted each of these issues into natural categories and created our fishbone.

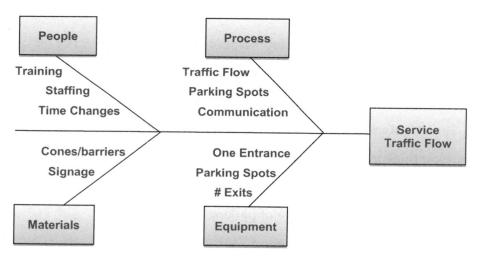

So which of the issues can you reasonably address?

- ✓ Training
- ✓ Staffing
- ✓ Service Time Overlap
- ✓ Police Communication
- ✓ Flow of Traffic
- ✓ Parking Spots

✓ Signage

✓ Cones

Some of these issues you can affect, but some you can't. For example, there's nothing you can do quickly about having one entrance to the church campus, but there are definitely some other things you can do to improve the parking situation.

Action Plan

Let's now look at all of the issues you identified and put a plan in place to fix the ones you can.

When I help teams do a plan like this, I think it's really important to not only determine what we need to do but also to assign responsibility to specific people to ensure they do it. And writing it down helps people remember!

It's also helpful to determine a due date for completion of the assigned tasks so that there's some accountability attached to it, and everyone understands the deadline.

Service Traffic Flow Action Plan				
Issue	Action Steps	Responsible Person	Due Date	Status Update
Training	Develop and schedule training for volunteers and police officers.	Steve Jones	May 1	Completed
Staffing	Work with volunteer coordinator to recruit additional parking volunteers.	Stacy Smith	June15	In Process
Service Time Overlap	Work with service coordinator to assess service time overlap.	Steve Jones Tom Jackson	May 1	Completed
Police Communication	Speak with lead police officer to improve police communications.	Steve Jones	May 1	Completed
Flow of Traffic	Work with facilities to change direction of traffic flow.	Steve Jones Jack Thompson	May 15	In Process
Parking Spots	Work with facilities to add parking spots.	Steve Jones Jack Thompson	May 15	In Process
Signage	Order new signage to reflect changes.	Steve Jones	May 15	In Process
Cones	Order additional parking cones.	Steve Jones	May 15	In Process
Traffic Flow Time	Re-measure traffic flow time.	Steve Jones	July 1	In process
Single Entrance	Add additional entrance to long-term facility plan.	Steve Jones	May 1	Completed

As you can see in this example action plan, we use five columns to organize the information.

The first column identifies the issue we're going to address; the next column describes what we need to do (action steps) to address the issue.

We then assign responsibility to someone to complete the action steps. We also assign a due date, and a column for status update helps us keeps track of each action step and how it's progressing.

Issues

We can identify issues through the fishbone exercise (or other brainstorming methods) and can prioritize based on available resources (people, time and money).

Action Steps/Responsible Person

The action steps come from brainstorming the necessary steps needed to address the issue. Sometimes it requires a single step, but other issues require a series of steps.

When determining action steps, I like to use a flipchart and let the team discuss the issue and

> "Success on any major scale requires you to accept responsibility. In the final analysis, the one quality that all successful people have...is the ability to take responsibility."
> Michael Korda

brainstorm steps to help address the issue. Simply ask the question and allow the group to discuss and agree on steps.

For example, I would ask the question, "What is it that we need to do to improve our volunteers and police training?" This question prompts a discussion that not only flushes out the necessary steps but also identifies who in the group is the best person to take responsibility for those steps. This is a group activity, and allowing the team to draft the plan ensures buy-in and support for its implementation.

Due Dates

When assigning due dates, I like to give the responsible person the opportunity to help determine a reasonable time frame to complete the task. This allows that person to take into consideration other time commitments so we won't impose an unrealistic timeline. This also means the action plan due date is merely a reminder of a timeline agreed and committed to.

So I would ask the question, "So, Steve, since we have determined you're the best person to complete these tasks, when do you think you can reasonably do them?" In this situation, Steve might look at his calendar and suggest a date. As long as the date is within reason, I just recommend we go with that date. If he gives an unreasonably long deadline, according to the group, we continue discussing and either help him become comfortable with a shorter timeline or look for another person who can complete the task sooner.

The goal is to get the tasks completed as soon as possible without pushing the limits on unreasonable expectations for volunteers.

Status Update

The status update column is what makes this a working document. Update the document before every team meeting and dedicate the first part of the meeting to status updates. This includes helping team members address barriers that may have kept them from completing a task.

For example, let's say Steve is responsible for developing the training for volunteers and police officers and is not getting the support from the volunteer office to contact and schedule the training. The team leader may have to intervene to try to find a solution.

Barriers to completing tasks is a common problem so it's important that the team lead helps to remove those barriers and helps keep the process moving along.

As you can see, this is a plan to address all of the issues. The most challenging issue, however, is only having one entrance for the church parking lot. We need to incorporate that fix into some of the long-term facility planning processes.

At this point, we begin to implement each of these steps and to monitor the traffic flow as we introduce some of these steps.

Once we do this, we can monitor the flow again and can determine whether these improvements are working or needs tweaking.

How do we do this?

Write Policy

The first thing we need to do is write policy and procedures for the new process. Writing it down and putting it in print solidifies the process. This also serves as a tool to

> "The best inspector is a well-designed process."
> Joseph M. Juran

use to remind volunteers and employees about the new process, but we can also use it as a training tool.

Suggestion: When writing the new policy, add an effective date for full implementation of the changes. This allows ample time to communicate the policy and train on its use.

Communicate Policy

Once we write the policy, we now want to communicate the policy to all stakeholders. In this example, that's employees, volunteers, and police officers.

When communicating process changes like this, it's a good practice to explain **why** you made the change. So, the explanation is that you made the change because of the feedback you were receiving from members and volunteers. Sharing this information helps everyone understand the why behind the change and fosters trust and buy-in.

Train on Policy

Next, you want to train everyone on the practical steps of the new policy. For traffic mitigation, this might include showing the team where supplies are, giving them a script of possible answers for angry motorists, and perhaps walking through the parking lot and showing them the new process.

> "Excellence must continue to increase and if it does not, it is no longer excellent and it will quickly become status quo."
> Phil Baker

After the training is complete, assign a few lead volunteers to help reinforce the training and help volunteers and police with questions about the changes.

Then incorporate the new process into new volunteer training for parking volunteers and police officers.

Accountability

Policies are only effective when people are accountable for adhering to them. For the traffic control problem, assign someone to observe and facilitate volunteers and police officers through the transition. This person should also give feedback up and down the line on policy compliance.

Review Policy Annually

Review every policy on an annual basis and modify as needed. These changes and modifications should then go through the same original steps to ensure everyone is on the same page and performs tasks consistently.

Assuming all your efforts are working, you have now created a new system and process for controlling parking flow. This again is doing the **right** thing **right** the **first time** and every time.

Chapter 9 – Next Steps

Now it's up to you to practice in your own environment. Identify some problems or processes that need improvement and gather a team to begin working on them. Make sure you include your volunteers and church members.

To do this:

Gather a team

Brainstorm problems within your church from the perspective of your key stakeholders: employees, volunteers, and church members.

Practice the fishbone

Use the **affinity** exercise to sort the issues into categories and draw the fishbone so you can have a picture of what the problem looks like. Have the team identify the reasons (people, material, process, equipment) for the problem. Brainstorm and come up with issues to address.

Develop an action plan

Use the issues identified in the fishbone to develop your action plan. Use the team to identify action steps, to assign the responsible person for completing those steps, and to draw up a timeline for completion.

Implement the plan

Implement the plan within the agreed to timeline.

Check results

If it works, write the policy, communicate it, and train the responsible parties. If it doesn't work, go through the process again. Some things to remember as you begin this process:

- First, it's important to get employee and volunteer involvement in any improvement effort. They're on the front lines and know better than anyone what the issues are.
- Start small and target two to three improvement projects to begin with.
- Target the low hanging fruit or, in other words, target those quick fixes first. This will help to create momentum and give the process creditability.
- Start small and practice going through the PDCA cycle.
- Follow through, follow through, follow through. There are many failed efforts out there because the team failed to follow through. And you're almost better off not starting an improvement initiative if you don't finish it. Starting and stopping is discouraging to the team and damages credibility.

What's in It for Me?

So what's in for me, you ask? I can only assume that if you're reading this book, you're on some level of church leadership. And since you're in a church leadership position, you can help your church, you get to experience teamwork, and you can enjoy the satisfaction that comes with working toward and achieving a shared goal. You can also take pride in participating in improving your church.

Last, it's an honor to have responsibility managing God's resources. So, to say we **get to** do this is pretty amazing!

About the Author

Patricia Lotich, MBA, is the founder of Smart Church Management and Thriving Small Business. As a business management consultant, Patricia helps organizations put systems and processes in place to manage their limited resources.

Also, she served as a business administrator for 10 years and has a driving passion to help churches fulfill their call by managing their God-given resources – people, time, and money.

Patricia is also a SCORE business counselor in southwest Florida and author of several books:

Smart Church Management: A Quality Approach to Business
    Administration

Smart Volunteer Management: A Volunteer Coordinator's
Handbook   for Engaging, Motivating, and Developing Volunteers

Church Staff Evaluations: A Guide to Performance Appraisals that
    Motivate, Develop, and Reward Church Employees.

All books are available on Amazon.

Websites:

SmartChurchManagement.com

ThrivingSmallBusiness.com

Contact:

Patricia@SmartChurchManagement.com

About Smart Church Management

Smart Church Management (SCM) is a church operations and management consulting company that offers services to help the local church, small businesses, and nonprofit organizations develop systems and processes to support development and growth.

Whether the system is to manage and budget limited resources; recruit, train, and schedule volunteers; or improve the process of hiring, training, and developing employees, SCM strives to help organizations manage their day-to-day operations.

If you would like to learn how Smart Church Management can help your organization, please contact SCM at:

Email: **info@smartchurchmanagement.com**

Phone: 314-229-4147

Additional References

Collins, Jim, *Good to Great: Why Some Companies Make the Leap and Others Don't*, HarperCollins Publishers, 2001

Evans, J.R., and Lindsay, W.M., *The Management and Control of Quality*, 6th edition, Cengage Learning, 2004.

LaFasto, F., and Larson C., *When Teams Work Best: 6,000 Team Members and Leaders Tell What It Takes to Succeed*, Sage Publications, 2001.

Maxwell, J.C., *The 21 Irrefutable Laws of Leadership: Follow Them and People Will Follow You*, 10th anniversary edition, Maxwell, John C. Thomas Nelson, 2007.

Stanley, Andy, *Deep & Wide: Creating Churches Unchurched People Love to Attend*, Zondervan, 2012

Warren, R., *The Purpose Driven Church: Every Church Is Big in God's Eyes*, Zondervan Publishing House, 1995.

Westcott, R.T., *The Certified Manager of Quality/Organizational Excellence*, ASQ Quality Press, 2005.